I Met Him Once

DR. LINDA KAY SMITH

as outlined by

Pastor Robert G. Smith

Copyright © 2014, Free Them Ministries, Inc.

All rights reserved.

ISBN: **978-0966338447**
ISBN-10: **0966338448**

King James Version of scriptures used due to public domain.

DEDICATION

Dedicated to my late husband and pastor, Robert G. Smith, who left this prophetic outline for me to find after he went Home. Dedicated also to the people of PowerHouse Christian Center, whom he loved.

CONTENTS

ACKNOWLEDGMENTS vii

1 WHEN I WAS LOST 1

2 WHEN I WAS AFRAID 5

3 WHEN I WAS LONELY 9

4 WHEN I WAS SICK 13

5 WHEN I WAS CONFUSED 17

6 WHEN I WAS MISTAKEN 21

7 WHEN I WAS IN ERROR 25

8 WHEN I WAS LOSING 27

9 WHEN I WAS FRIENDLESS 31

10 WHEN I WAS ANGRY 35

11 WHEN I WAS LYING 39

12 WHEN I WAS DRUNK 41

13 WHEN I WAS POOR 43

EPILOGUE 47

ABOUT THE AUTHOR 49

ACKNOWLEDGMENTS

About a week after my husband's death, I found the outline for this book. I didn't know he created it. The outline was apparently inspired by a patio conversation about meeting Jesus. We agreed that it wasn't just about salvation.

From the purely professional standpoint of publishing guidelines, the outline could be edited, made better, more succinct. However, I am choosing to honor what 'Pashur' Bob, as the children at church called him, left for me. I believe it is prophetic, having found it after his passing.

Each chapter is a double-edged sword. Each can be seen from a negative side or as a learning experience. Both will be presented; you choose.

Choose wisely.

1 WHEN I WAS LOST

How many evangelists have asked, "Have you met Jesus?"

Of course this is the starting point. For most of us, we can clearly remember the moment the 'salvation message' pierced our heart causing us to confess Jesus as our Lord. We responded with a resounding 'yes' to His invitation.

What about those who responded with a negative? They refused His sacrifice, His love. Both those who said yes and those who refused met the Savior. Their choice had the power to permanently alter their eternal standing.

I have met individuals who have no clear memory of when they became children of God through salvation. I suppose it's possible, but I have always wondered or rather marveled that such a significant moment wasn't more memorable. I remember my moment *very* clearly.

At one of the lowest points of my life, I was doing the mundane chore of frying chicken. I had rolled the television into the kitchen. When the next program came on it was during a critical moment in the frying and I could not change the channel just yet. The Billy Graham Crusade was being broadcast.

Normally I would have leapt over furniture to turn off Rev. Graham's program. I didn't want to hear the worshipful singing. I didn't want to hear the scriptures and I didn't want to watch as those poor pitiful people made their way down to give up their lives, their choices, their fun in exchange for God's oppressive lordship (or so I thought).

As I said, the chicken demanded my attention, and before I realized it was happening I found myself on my knees accepting the call to salvation. The message had me and I met Jesus. I don't remember the exact words Rev. Graham used. I do remember feeling as though someone had looked inside my heart, physically! I felt exposed and vulnerable and I knew I needed help. I knew I needed a savior. Jesus filled the hole left by that supernatural surgery.

Bob had a slightly different experience. He was raised in a denomination that had confirmation (not Catholic) and as a child, he confessed Jesus as Lord. He said he clearly remembered that he really believed what he confessed. He understood it though he was a child. He was saved.

Years later, he did what was known as a rededication. I had been going to church for a while after my salvation experience and he would stay home. He said I could have been gone shopping for hours and it wouldn't have mattered, but the couple of hours I was gone to church were the loneliest he had ever felt. So, he began to accompany me, rededicating his life to the Lord.

For both of us there were many years of living as though these moments didn't occur, but in Heaven, God knew we belonged to Him and Him alone. We had to learn *how* to *be* Christians, not just *about* being Christians.

Several years later, we were blessed to attend the revival at Brownsville Assembly of God. Our lives would never be the same and the transformation was equally significant in our hearts, mind and souls as was our salvation experience.

I am saddened that so many Christians never knew the revival at Brownsville even occurred. I realized not everything that is called a revival truly is a revival, but for us, Brownsville was the real deal. We were also shocked that there were Christians that went there and experienced nothing special. We were truly changed for God's glory.

Salvation and revival combined, we went on to live Christian lives. We were all in for Jesus. That doesn't mean that we didn't make mistakes. It does mean that those mistakes were followed by true repentance. The sins became fewer and fewer as the commitment grew and grew.

If you have heard the call to salvation in your life, it means you met Jesus. If you did not accept the invitation at that time and if Jesus hasn't returned for His people before you read this book, there is still time.

Romans 10:9-10 KJV, That if thou shalt confess with thy mouth the Lord Jesus, and shalt believe in thine heart that God hath raised him from the dead, thou shalt be saved. For with the heart man believeth unto righteousness; and with the mouth confession is made unto salvation.

Do it. Say it and mean it, "Jesus, you are my Lord."

It will be a second meeting with the King of Kings and the Lord of Lords. He's been waiting for you. Then never stop meeting with Him. You will have begun a relationship that blossoms when you spend time with Jesus. Salvation is not a one-time even, it is a continuing experience.

2 WHEN I WAS AFRAID

Every person on the planet has probably been truly afraid once in their life. We have a lot of pseudonyms for fear; stage fright, nightmares, phobia, panic attacks, etc.

I have a healthy empathy concerning fear. Fear was a constant companion since childhood and there were legitimate causes for fear.

Fear caused me to consider suicide, but fear also drove me to Jesus. I better explain. The same week I saw the Billy Graham Crusade and became a Christian I had another experience I now know was supernatural.

Because of early childhood events, I had developed a strong fear of nighttime and of basements. As an adult I knew this fear was ridiculous, but there it was. So that same week, while alone in the house, the fear swelled to a crescendo. I just knew the 'monster' was in the basement.

I decided I just couldn't live that afraid one more night. I was going to kill the monster or it would kill me. Either way the fear would end. So with knife in hand, I started toward the basement.

It was then that I heard a voice. It said, "Find your Bible."

I had no idea if I had a Bible or where it might be, but I was drawn to my bedside table. There, under all the questionable literature, I found it, the 'Holy Bible'. It was the red letter edition that was used by my mother to help me learn to read. It had gold edging on the pages and a wonderful zipper that held everything in safety when closed.

I had abandoned the knife (temporarily, or so I thought) and heard the voice say, "Open it and read."

My eyes fell on a scripture, "This then is the message which we have heard of Him, and declare unto you, that God is light, and in Him is no darkness at all." (1 John 1:5)

Remember, I was terrified of the night, the darkness and particularly the dark basement. The 'voice' had somehow led me to the perfect comforting words. I was meeting Jesus.

The voice then said, "Turn the page."

The next passage read, "There is no fear in love; but **perfect love** casteth out fear: because fear hath torment. He that feareth is not made perfect in love."

The voice had managed, once again, to lead me to the perfect comfort, perfect love. I had met Jesus.

I learned in subsequent studies that fear is caused by the spirit of fear which is not from God and that God gave me power, love and a sound mind. (2 Timothy 1:7)

It was many years before I found out there were times my husband was afraid. Like many men, he 'protected' me from seeing his fear. But, what I also found out was that he took his fear to God and God loved it away.

Some parents find alternative ways to relieve a child's fear. Perhaps they leave a nightlight on or provide them with a special stuffed animal to clutch or let them sleep in Mommy's and Daddy's bed.

I believe when we do this, we miss an opportunity to let them meet Jesus. Only a loving Savior has *perfect* love. Therefore, only the Loving Savior can rid us of the fear.

Nightlights, stuffed animals and someone else's bed are no substituted for the embrace of our Heavenly Father. Help them meet Jesus.

As a pastor and Christian counsellor, I have talked with people about their fears. There is always a root cause that allowed the Spirit of fear to enter in a make a home in the mind. The method is sure. Show them how much they are loved by Jesus and introduce them to the One who loved them unconditionally. They meet Jesus, perhaps for the first time.

Because fear is a spirit and a tool of the adversary, the devil, there will be times throughout your Christian walk when the enemy tempts you with fear. These will not necessarily be the times you are spiritually strong. These temptations come during times of trials. They are added like salt in an open wound.

When my husband died, although I had overcome fear before, I was once again challenged with the spirit of fear. Like many Americans in this economy, we were unable to afford life insurance so when my husband died, my finances were under attack as well. The enemy saw the opportunity and here came the spirit of fear.

It took prayer, faith, Christian friends, scripture, more prayer, the blood of the Lamb and my testimony, and a little time, but I overcame the spirit of fear once again.

Many times, God has told believers, "Fear not."

Even at the conception of Jesus, Mary and Joseph had to be told not to fear. The shepherds, on the night Jesus was born, were told not to fear. We can see that satan uses fear to try to stop powerful moves of God.

This is reason to rejoice in fear. Paul said to rejoice when we fall into various temptations knowing that the trying of our faith works patience. Patience helps us wait while God works out the solution to our situation.

God has and is still showing me the solution to my finances. God has supplied by need according to riches in glory by Christ Jesus. God has not forsaken me. God has prepared a table before me in the presence of my enemies. What I have just written is all from scripture. The answer to fear is found in God's Word.

Jesus is the Word made flesh. Meet Jesus. Fear will leave.

3 WHEN I WAS LONELY

First, let's admit there's a difference between being alone and being lonely. Some people thrive on solitude. They are happy with their own company and nature or some other environment.

In this chapter, we are speaking of the emotional void we may feel due to the lack of relationship, intimacy, friendship. It's the feeling that something is missing that would make us happy or whole.

One of the most well-known scriptures about being lonely or rather, alone is found in the book of Genesis when the Godhead said it was not good for man to be alone. Of course, in that case God was indicating and Adam needed Eve. What we should take from that is God knows what we need. God can and will provide what we need.

Loneliness is not always a physical condition. You may have heard it said you can be lonely in a crowd. There are as many causes of loneliness as there are people on the planet. Some of the more common causes would be a violent separation as in the cases of divorce, death or abandonment.

Loneliness can also be caused by soul wounds such as an orphan spirit, spirit of rejection, separation caused by bitterness or a lack of forgiveness. Most of our attempts to cure loneliness are simply a Band-Aid and are ill conceived. Only God can fix the root of the problem.

If the problem can't be reversed (death, for example), God will heal the wound and make a way to recover, driving out the loneliness. I can hear a thought in my head, "But, I will always miss (Insert Name Here)."

Missing someone and loneliness are two different conditions. I could be with most of my friends and one friend not be in the crowd and we will miss the one. That does not mean we are lonely.

There is a wholeness that only comes from a relationship with our Lord and Savior, Jesus Christ. Before I was saved and began to learn about Jesus, I was most miserably lonely. I had friends, I had parents and siblings, I had a husband, but someone was missing.

Jesus heard my cry and filled that emptiness. God said, in several places in scripture that God would never leave us or forsake us. That is absolutely true. I am always aware of God. Even when tempted by the enemy, satan, to think God was angry or disappointed in me, I knew God loved me and was there somewhere. Perhaps I had distanced myself, but God was just a faithful thought away.

The woman at the well (Samaritan Woman) probably felt lonely. She had been with several men, but there was something different about the man at the well. Sure, he told her all she had ever done, but it was more than that. He *saw* her. He really saw her as a person with some worth about her. He showed her kindness.

David said, in a Psalm, that he realized even if he could make his bed in hell, God would be there. David asked the Lord to never take the Lord's presence from him. Of course, God loves David and has never left him.

The scriptures teach us that when we are born again, that is, we have confessed Jesus is our Lord and we believe God raised Him from the dead (Romans 10:9-10), that we have Christ in us. (Colossians 1:27)

Therefore, it is impossible to actually be lonely ever again. I miss my late husband terribly. I miss by mom, my brother who have both passed away. I miss friends who are far away, but I can never truly be lonely again for Jesus is always with me.

Jesus will be with me eternally.

True emotional loneliness is, I believe, a problem with 'self'. The two great commandments tell us to love God and then to love our neighbors as ourselves. Many people struggle with loving themselves. If I do not love me, I can't truly love another.

This lack of loving ourselves causes a cruel loneliness. We will lack fulfillment and peace if we can't find it in another person. It is really not fair to expect someone else to do what we won't, that is, love us. As a pastor, I refuse to perform a wedding for two broken people who are trying to make a whole. It won't work. They are doomed for failure.

In order to have truly successful relationships, we start with ourselves, allowing Jesus to heal, restore, and make us whole. Only then are we prepared to enter into covenant relationship as in a marriage.

You've no doubt seen a husband and wife in a restaurant, sitting across from each other, one reading a paper, one on the cell phone, no talking. This can be a sure sign of loneliness. Although there is another person there, the relationship is missing.

Because Jesus was tempted in all points as we are, Jesus also was tempted to experience loneliness. However, in John 16 he said that while people may abandon him, God would never abandon him so he would never be alone.

Are you lonely, even in a crowd? Do you struggle with loving yourself? There is a friend who sticks closer than a brother. That friend is Jesus. He's waiting to meet you.

4 WHEN I WAS SICK

Long before I met the Healer, God was keeping me alive. Born with a rare birth defect, I was constantly being treated for various infections, and was sometimes at the point of death.

My mother, though not a woman of strong faith, would simply pray, sometimes all night. Miraculously, I would recover. When I was struck by a car as a child, mother prayed and I recovered.

All this recovering happened when I was not aware of being a Christian. Now, as a born again Christian I have seen believers pray for the sick. Sometimes there were miraculous recoveries and healing, but sometimes healing didn't come.

By faith, I believe scriptures that teach by the stripes of Jesus Christ we were healed. I believe God when God says, "I am the One who heals your disease." I can't explain every circumstance of people not being healed. I can't explain why rank sinners are healed but a Christian might not be healed. I just know healing is provided through Jesus Christ and accessed by faith or God's mercy.

I remember one particular time that fits this chapter. For some unknown reason, I became extremely sick. I had very high fevers and couldn't eat or get out of bed except for excruciating trips to the toilet. I stayed in that bed for several days. I was sometimes delirious.

My husband would come check on me bringing me water and aspirin. He tried to get me to eat, but I took nothing for at least three days or more. He kept asking me to let him take me to the hospital. I refused. When he finally insisted that I was going to the emergency room, I yelled at him saying, "You will NOT remove me from this bed! God will heal me or I will die here."

The next day I recovered. I got up, washed, ate and rested. Jesus met me at that point of faith. That same husband would later die in that same bed even though we prayed constantly for his recovery. Why? Why did I experience healing and he did not?

Some would say he *was* healed. He was just healed in Heaven while I was healed here. That's cute. Sounds good. I still desire understanding. I want to be able, as a preacher, to give a definite explanation rather that guess at the mind of God or the spiritual health of the individual as risk.

What I do know is I can point to times in my own life where I met Jesus when I was sick and Jesus healed me. With the birth defect, I am not supposed to be alive and even alive, I am supposed to be on oxygen, mostly an invalid, yet none of that is the case. I preach, I travel, and I live a normal supernatural life.

I will never stop believing God heals.

I could write a very academic book on the subject of healing. I could tell you that some diseases are caused by inward demonic activity. I could show you that the environment in which we live causes illness, but God has given us promises about protection from our environment.

Though I show you a thousand scriptures, still not everyone will manifest healing. I just keep coming back to faith. By faith I *know* God heals.

Recently some Christians posted on a social media site, foods we should not eat and foods we should eat that would cure cancer. I will agree we could all eat healthier. What I see is desperation to accomplish what it looks like God is not doing, stopping cancer.

God did stop cancer thousands of years ago in the crucifixion and resurrection of Jesus Christ. Essentially, that was my reply on the social media site. Eat or don't eat certain foods. Exercise or not. Without Jesus you can forget about healing.

I believe it is God who inspires discoveries in medicine, and breakthroughs in treatments and prevention.

I may have had surgeries, taken antibiotics or had therapies in the past, but make no mistake, it is Jesus who healed me by His stripes. I will always give the glory to Him for my healing.

Some of you may have chronic conditions. I encourage you to keep meeting Jesus in your condition. We have too much evidence in scripture of healing for chronic conditions to doubt God's willingness and ability to heal.

Another cute phrase we use to describe Jesus' healing power is to call Him 'the Great Physician'. No! Jesus is the great healer, not only of our bodies, but of our souls. Introduce your illness to Jesus and watch it flee.

5 WHEN I WAS CONFUSED

I wish I could ask my husband about this chapter title. He always seemed so sure of himself, so confident in God. I would not have thought he was confused. I supposed all humans are confused at some point so let's look at that subject.

Returning to the safe harbor of scripture, we learn that God is not the author of confusion. That means satan is the author of confusion. I could go on a theological expedition here and give you many verses about not being double minded, letting your 'eye' be single, having the mind of Christ, and taking your thoughts captive. The bottom line is, if we are confused, we need to meet Jesus once again.

Every person whom God reveals to us in scripture had at least a moment of confusion so I don't think it surprises God that we have trouble figuring out things occasionally. God knows that our thoughts engage in battle with one another.

I can almost laugh when I think about Paul calling himself a wretched man only to later call himself an apostle in charge of the care of all the churches in Asia. He would then turn around and say he was the least.

Adam was confused about the temptation in the Garden in Eden and about which voice to listen to. David was confused about Bathsheba and also about Saul's dislike for him. Jonah was confused about prophesying to Nineveh. Peter was confused about several things. It happens.

However, when I consider Jesus, the confusion must go. The purity of my Lord drives it away. The absolutes of scripture are comforting. They bring balance and order.

I have had several dear sisters in the Lord who would say to me, "Well, what does the Word say?" This was the question when discussing a point of confusion. This is where we meet Jesus once again. Jesus is the Word made flesh.

In the midst of confusion, the enemy strives to keep us from reading the Word of God. Our brains want to mull over the situation. Around and around the thoughts go and they never seem to rest.

This is the precise moment we need to rendezvous with our Lord, the Living Word of God. What does the Word say? What would Jesus do? Once we know that, we know what we should say and do.

One passage I love so much is found in Hebrews 13:5 and 6. "Let your conversation be without covetousness; and be content with such things as ye have: **for he hath said**, I will never leave thee, nor forsake thee. <u>So that we may boldly say</u> , The Lord is my helper, and I will not fear what man shall do unto me."

He has said so that we may boldly say . . .

He has said so that *I* may BOLDLY say . . .

When we meet Jesus concerning the subject of our confusion, He speaks to us and then we boldly decree what He speaks. Confusion goes!

Confusion leaving does not mean we have the entire detailed answer to our situation, but we will have peace during the trial. The peace is not always understandable, but it is such a blessed relief. We can then stop the circling confusing thoughts. We can breathe once again and relax into God's care. It literally feels like casting our anxiety onto Him. (1 Peter 5:7)

An early Bible teacher of my husband and I told us if, in any situation, we did not know what to do, DO NOTHING!

There have been so many situations in which keeping this rule kept us from making major mistakes. If my husband and I disagreed on a course of action, we waited. We did nothing. We prayed and waited for the revelation in the situation.

Eventually and never late, the answer would come to one or both of us simultaneously. Even if only one of us saw the solution from God, the other knew in our Spirit the answer was correct. The proof was the situation would work out for our good because we loved the Lord and are called according to His purpose.

Confusion brings no glory to God. The God solution will always bring God glory. This is a great measuring stick, so to speak. If we act prematurely out of our impatience or frustration when we are confused, we will surely mess things up.

Along with finding the God answer in the midst of confusion, we need to deal with the source of the confusion, satan. The Bible tells us to resist the devil and he will flee. Draw close to God and God will draw close to you.

When we are confused, we must resist the confusion at its source. Tell satan to go and take confusion with satan. We have the power, in Jesus' name to rebuke. The Word of God is profitable for rebuke. (2 Timothy 3:16)

Remember Jesus' responses on the Mt. of Temptation? The devil would try to bring in confusion and Jesus would say, "It is written."

Eventually the devil fled taking confusion with him.

Confusion tries to get us to forget who we are in Christ Jesus. When we lose our God-identity, we can't see the next step. Scripture says God orders the steps of a righteous person. Righteousness and confusion are at odds with each other.

Jesus is the author and finisher of our faith. In the midst of confusion, we look at Jesus. We remember who we are and whose we are. We are no longer confused for, once again, we have met Jesus.

6 WHEN I WAS MISTAKEN

My husband saw a difference between a mistake, an error and a lie. We will look at error and lies in later chapters. Being mistaken to him, was when you thought you had the right information and spoke or acted on that, but it turned out you had the wrong information.

This may not seem like a big deal to some, but he was mortified over the negative effect his words or actions may have had on someone just because he didn't check his facts.

For me I see this the most in teaching or preaching the Word of God.
We are all constantly refining our understanding of God's word, but as a young student minister, I just innocently and blindly believed everything my instructors said about Theology or Divinity. Their views went unchallenged.

I finally began to understand it was important to check things out myself. Scripture that is researched free from tradition/doctrine of men and from regurgitated data, is glorious! It is the birthplace of revelation.

Before I learned that truth, I taught concepts I now know were incorrect or at least not as perfected as they could have been. I regret the misinformation and the ignorance it sowed in those listening to me. It was a time when I was mistaken.

Rumors are usually mistaken information. What passes for news nowadays is often at least a mistake causing a later correction or rescinding of the original reporting.

Why is this something to be concerned about? When we act or speak on misinformation and a lack of understanding, we set results into motion. Misinformation has caused accidents, divorces, suicides, bad investments and a host of unfortunate repercussions.

I have a dear friend who once thought I didn't like her. She had respect for me as a teacher of the Word, and wanted to be friends, but thought I considered myself above her.

She was mistaken. In fact, I also wanted to be friends. I was mistaken as well for I thought her reluctance was rejection. Many years later we realized we were mistaken and discovered we actually grew up very near one another and that her mother and my aunt made quilts together.

I have babysat her son, she has gone on ministry trips with me and we have long wonderful phone conversations.

All we would have had to do initially is get the correct information. Either one of us could have easily approached the other and said we would like to be friends.

Misinformation causes mistakes. Mistakes cause problems.

My husband and I had many discussions about the difference between mistakes, errors and lies. We didn't always agree. So, what is to be done? I have to ask, "Well, what does the word say?"

The older English versions of scripture do not use the term 'mistake' or 'mistaken'. However, some later transliterations do use that word.

One Hebrew word that could be translated 'mistake' is *mishgeh*. It means something was an oversight, but it also means to mislead. One definition say it means to err. (I can almost hear my husband trying to explain the subtle differences now).

The point of all this is, when we make a mistake, it's Jesus to the rescue! Whether it's a mistake or an error, Jesus is there with forgiveness. Jesus is our advocate with the Father.

I was just reminded of the incident on the road to Emmaus. At first the travelers thought Jesus was just some guy. They didn't recognize Him. They were mistaken. As He spoke to them they sensed something different about Him. Later they realized their mistake. He was Jesus! How did they not see that?

Up to a certain point they had just hearsay about the events of the resurrecti on day. They knew some women had told them they couldn't find the body and that some other apostles went and checked it out and they couldn't find the body either. It took spending time with Jesus to clear the mistaken information.

They finally got it right. Jesus is alive! Their hearts burned in them hearing Him teach the Word of God. Jesus corrected the mistake and then some!

My grandmother had several children, all of who were mischievous. When there was trouble she wouldn't bother with details. They *all* got a whipping. This lack of information was also a mistake because it frustrated justice. While the offender did indeed get punishment, he or she also got the thrill of seeing others punished for their deed.

Scripture tells us God's people are destroyed for lack of knowledge. Of course this can mean lack of knowledge of the Word of God, but we can also be destroyed by lack of knowledge in any area.

We need to slow down, get the facts, get wisdom from above and then speak or act. Explaining, "I didn't know," won't cut it. Wisdom from above has peace and is easy to carry out. It doesn't have partiality. (James 3:17)

Jesus made it possible for us to have Holy Spirit present in our daily lives. Holy Spirit leads us and guides us into all truth. Holy Spirit knows things we do not know and through Holy Spirit, we have Word of Knowledge and Word of Wisdom.

This knowledge will help us stay mistake free.

7 WHEN I WAS IN ERROR

First of all, see chapter 6. Have you ever said, "I should have known better."?

Error is when an action is taken that is out of its proper time. It does not follow the specific instructions of God. It is well-intentioned, but misses the mark in some small way. This wasn't done out of rebellion. Sometimes it's out of zeal, impatience or unsanctified mercy.

There is a Greek word in the New Testament that could mean error. It is *hamartia*. Although it is not exactly worded this way in Strong's Concordance, *hamartia* means missing the mark in thought, word and/or deed. It is sometimes translated as sin, but let me remind you that to God, if we know to do good and don't do it, it is sin to us.

Perhaps an example is needed. Let's say an exuberant young minister reads the passage, Mark 16:15- 16, And he said unto them, Go ye into all the world, and preach the gospel to every creature. He that believeth and is baptized shall be saved; but he that believeth not shall be damned.

The young minister doesn't compare scripture to scripture, doesn't check Matthew 28:19-20, and doesn't check out the original language, apply it with the law of love, and seek God's guidance and then act.

So the young minister jumps up, gets on the computer, orders a plane ticket to somewhere in China, Africa, the Congo, South America, gets on the plain and starts evangelizing in the streets. Sounds holy, right? Problem is the town where the minister lives is also part of the world. God had a specific place and time in mind. We call it a divine appointment. The young minister, in his or her (I bet a lot of you were automatically thinking it was a man) zeal missed the mark.

Perhaps God was setting up some things on the other end. Perhaps God had a different assignment. Perhaps the minister was supposed to pastor and not run all over the world.

What the minister did was not bad, just not quite right. It wasn't in God's timing or perfected plan for this minister. He or she was in error.

As the minister grows in spiritual maturity, they will learn to wait upon the Lord and download the specifics for their assignment and then act.

Sometimes in unsanctified mercy, we try to help someone in a manner we choose rather than what God chose. I see this often with parents and grandparents. God is merciful and we are supposed to have compassion for others, but if our merciful acts are not directed by God, we can metaphorically treat a severed limb with a Band-Aid.

God's timing and method are crucial to success. Sarah, Abraham's wife, had Ishmael outside of God's timing and source. She grew weary waiting on the promise of God and forced the situation. When people repeat this error, I call it an Ishmael. Ishmael's are not bad, they are just not God's best. Creating an Ishmael is usurping God's way.

God said God's ways are higher than our ways. Come up higher. Jesus only did what He saw the Father do and only said what He heard Father say. It's a good example.

8 WHEN I WAS LOSING

You may have seen someone, hopefully just a child, make an 'L' with their fingers on one hand, hold it to their forehead and say, "Loser!"

Of course, the person doing that doesn't make it so, but what the enemy knows is this; somewhere in each of us is a seed of self-doubt. Perhaps we *are* a loser.

We may have had moments of victory in our life and we may now be fairly self-confident. Somewhere, sometime you felt like a loser. You may even have a soul wound concerning this self-image. Only in Christ is it possible to heal soul wounds and develop confidence in God that will sustain the onslaught of the enemy.

Self-doubt can be utilized as fertile soil for the seeds of salvation. At the moment a person doesn't know who they really are or what is their purpose is the perfect time for a believer to witness to them. They need to build a new identity in Christ Jesus. They need to know what their purpose is in God's kingdom.

Ecclesiastes 12:13 tells us the whole duty of man is to reverence God and keep God's commandments. That assignment is easier than trying to prove our success in society. God loves you. Society doesn't love you. It's easier to please God than to please people.

We sometimes feel like a loser because we have suffered an injustice. Jesus, according to scripture, is our advocate, our mediator. Jesus fights for our justice, reinforces our potential and secures our future. He is all victorious.

There's an old saying, 'you can't fight City Hall.' That's true sometimes, but Jesus *can* fight for us. Jesus can even avenge us. That is true victory and we are more than a conqueror in Christ Jesus.

Once, when I was about ten to twelve years old, my mother said, "You never finish anything. You are a quitter."

Those wounds flew into my soul like a cruel arrow and stuck. Over the years, my mother had said kind things, encouraging things and other mean things to me, but these words were poisoned by satan. Years later, as a Christian, I realized that Jesus had taken those words and shoved them right back in the devil's face. I had become an overcomer in Christ. As the apostle Paul, I was now a race finisher!

One of the horrible things parents, spouses, teachers, or employers can do to us is put losing labels on us. It may be true that an individual is lazy or a quitter, but labeling them out loud is akin to cutting with a sword.

The wounded individuals may go onto overcome the accusation, but we cannot credit the accuser for reverse psychological inspiration. Whether the overcomer realized it or not, God has aided and enabled them. Even if it's just a matter of the wonder of creation, we have in us the desire to live and live well.

Scripture tells us that in Christ, we are a new creature. Old things are passed away and all things become new. It is a 'do over'. It is a 'clean slate'.

There are many stories of famous entertainers who had a music teacher tell them they couldn't sing well or play an instrument well. Many best-selling authors were told they couldn't write. Fortune 500 CEOs were drop outs of high school and told they would never amount to anything.

When talking about faith, the Bible says in Romans 4:17 that we should call those things that are not as though they were. I would also say, overcoming things that were called 'not' because they are not. (Needs better wording, but you get the idea.)

I became a finisher, thus dissolving the words that I was a quitter. Mother didn't inspire that turnaround. God took what satan meant for evil and turned it to good.

Find the loser words in your life that have hung you up. Give them to

God and watch the transformation!

One physical exercise that seems to help people be free from past hurtful words or actions is to take your hand as if you are reaching into your heart, pull out what has made you feel like a loser, place it in your other hand and throw it up to Jesus to deal with.

This may seem childish to you, but I assure you I have seen the positive emotional impact it has on people.

You can do all things through Christ Jesus which strengthens you. You can live as a winner and not a loser. God calls you victorious.

9 WHEN I WAS FRIENDLESS

An area that satan has perverted is the definition of friend. With the arrival of social media the word friend has been distorted and corrupted. When I see a corruption like this, I must return to the original language of scripture to find God's definition.

In Exodus 33:11, where God talks to Moses as a man talks to a friend, the word friend implies an intimacy rather than a passing acquaintance. By the way 'intimacy' is not sexual. That is another definition that has been distorted.

The root of the word for friend in scriptures is like being in the same herd, grazing in the same pasture. While there may be too much information given out in social media, it is not intimacy and it is among scattered people. These are not friends if all that is common in the computer.

I am friends with Christians around the world, but that is because we are all in the family of God, the household of faith. We are all sheep of His pasture and Jesus is the Great Shepherd of the sheep.

Because I have been a Christian minister for some time, all of my friends are found in the Church. This also means my highs and lows with friends have been experienced within the Church.

It has been said that when the chips are down you find out who your true friends are. I would say you find out who your close relatives are. Proverbs 17:17 reads, "A friend loves at all times, and a brother is born for adversity."

In the body of Christ your friends are your family and your family are your friends. God is our Father. When our friends act as close as family in the bad times, we experience true friendship. They can only do this because of the Christ in them. Only God can inspire them to sustain that kind of friendship.

I may not have understood this until I did go through adversity. Three times in my life I found out who true friends were. Once was when I was diagnosed with cancer. Once was when a dear pastor went into a life of sin and my home church disintegrated. Once was when my husband of 39 years, died.

The night before surgery to remove the cancer, I spent hours on the phone with a friend who loved me enough not to just agree with my whining. She talked truth to me. She was firm in her delivery. Just sympathizing with someone may not be the best way to be a good friend. God chastens whom God loves and this friend let me know in no uncertain terms that I was messed up in my thinking.

My pastor going into sin and my home church disintegrating was very devastating. This was the pastor who initially taught me about Christianity. All my friends, or so I thought, were in that church. All my Christian identity was held in those friendships. I was wrong to be in that situation.

The good that came from that is I re-evaluated all that I thought I knew about God, the Bible, salvation and friendships. I am happy to say that I do still have good friends all of who have left that church and gone on to live productive glorious Christian lives.

When my husband died I also experience Christian friendship in a deep way. When people participate in helping you through that trauma, not just in an occasional kind word, but in actions, you really appreciate true friendship.

In these times of heartache, true friends were evident. Many so called friends offered condolences and words of encouragement, but true friends went the extra mile. They were *there* in ways unexpected.

Jesus is like that and more. Jesus is with us always. Once Jesus takes us on, we are truly and forever His.

Jesus was *there* for us before we ever knew Him. He gave His life. No greater love has a man than to lay down his life for another.

True friends don't mind being inconvenienced when you really, really need them. True friends are sacrificial. True friends will tell you the truth even when you don't want to hear it.

Jesus is a true friend.

10 WHEN I WAS ANGRY

We all have our 'thing'. You know, that thing that you have to work at frequently, even after you are saved. For some of us the thing is 'anger'.

God absolutely knew we would have anger. Don't forget, God has things God doesn't like. God hates sin for example. Jesus displayed anger, but the Bible says Jesus was without sin. Remember, Jesus turned over tables outside of church! Wow! I would have thought that would be counted as sin.

God said in the scripture, "Be angry and sin not." So being angry is not a sin. It's what we do when we are angry that may be a sin. Jesus even called church leaders (Pharisees) vipers and hypocrites, yet this was not counted as sin to him. I must admit, that one is still a bit baffling to me.

When we are angry, the power that keeps us from sinning is meeting Jesus at the point of our anger. That truly is a 'what would Jesus do' moment. The control can only happen if we take a second between our anger and our action or words.

Too often I have had to apologize for words said in anger.

I don't think anyone truly appreciates the trauma caused when they lash out in anger. As a Christian counselor, I have spoken with many people who have emotional scars from anger-borne actions. People can clearly recall, years later, when a parent acted out in anger, perhaps hurting someone with physical violence or putting their fist through a wall.

I have shown several young husbands how they are simply repeating the pattern of their father in slamming around the house throwing things or hitting things. When they realized they can take control of their own lives and stop repeating the actions of their father, the relief is almost tangible.

We don't have to be taught anger. It is part of our Adam nature. Take a bottle away from a hungry infant and you will see anger. Tell a toddler 'no' and you will see anger.

The Bible does tell fathers not to provoke their children to anger. I would say that includes mothers as well. The opposite of not provoking to anger is NOT condoning every bad act. We do have to dispense proper discipline and set boundaries for our children.

Although we are not taught to be angry, we do learn reactions to our anger. You may have seen mom give everyone the silent treatment. Perhaps a sibling would storm out of the house and stay gone for hours. Then there's the more tragic examples of hurting animals or self-mutilation.

It is Jesus and the unconditional love He shares that can take the wind out of our sails when we are angry and calm us down. One look at that beautiful face, one beat from that beautiful heart and the rage stops.

The devil is not in the cause of the anger, the devil is in getting us out of control with the anger. Jesus calmed the raging see, the wild storm and Jesus can calm our mind, and emotions.

Jesus can show us acceptable ways to diffuse our anger. Walk it off. Pray. Speak in tongues. Whistle. Ask Holy Spirit to give you a plan, a system, a diffuser. For me, it was a comparison technique. I would look at what made me angry and compare it to what Jesus went through on the cross. The anger trigger became small by comparison.

Another method to curb my angry outbursts is to think, "If something truly tragic happened right now, I wouldn't care about this situation that is making me angry."

I learned that one when a dear brother died. Situations that would have made me angry before, meant nothing on that day. There was a stronger emotion taking over. Therefore, if the stronger emotion is love when we are tempted to act on anger, then the anger loses and the love wins.

It's anger vs love. God is love and vengeance is God's. Simply relax and let God balance things out. God will fight our battles. God will work it out.

Angry outbursts are usually a feeble attempt to control things when we feel out of control. When allowed to impose itself daily, this ager becomes abusive to those around us. Verbal abuse can be just as harmful and scarring as physical abuse.

A consistently angry parent can cripple a child's future, damage future relationships. A consistently angry parent is subconsciously teaching their child a pattern to be repeated as an adult. That parent is also wrecking the lives of their future son-in-law, daughter-in-law and grandchildren.

There is no need to exert angry control. Turn the control over to the Lord Jesus Christ. Let Him be Lord instead of you. Run to Him when you are angry. He's waiting for you.

DR. LINDA KAY SMITH

11 WHEN I WAS LYING

According to definition is scripture, a liar is one who speaks *deliberate* falsehood. Note the emphasis on 'deliberate'. This was a frequent point of discussion with my husband.

He thought if someone said something that wasn't truth, it was a lie. However, the key is whether it was deliberate or not. The Bible has an interesting phrase in Revelation 21:27, 'make a lie'. Again, this is an intentional falsehood. The intent is to deceive.

Since the Word of God is Truth and we are to worship God in Spirit and in Truth (John 4:24), we can see that Truth is really pretty important. Since the enemy, the devil, is the father of lies, we can appreciate what a slap in the face of God it would be to intentionally lie.

One of the assignments of Holy Spirit is to lead and guide us into all truth. Therefore, when we intentionally lie, it grieves Holy Spirit. But, what does our lie do to someone else?

When we intentionally deceive someone else we start a chain reaction that can have dire consequences for them or for ourselves. Let me give you what seems like a humorous example.

I knew a group of brothers who had the typical sibling rivalry going on. One day the two older brothers told a lie to the younger brother. They, over a period of the day, convinced him he could fly. They worked that lie and worked that lie intentionally deceiving their little brother.

You guessed it, by afternoon, they convinced him to jump off the barn vigorously flapping homemade 'wings'. The older boys knew full well he would crash to the ground and they would laugh and laugh.

However, when he hit the ground he was injured. An intentional lie causes an injury whether to the body or to the soul. Let me give you another example.

I knew a women whose mother passed away. When the family was clearing out her house days later, the woman found a sealed envelope, and written on the outside it said, "Destroy in the event of my death". Well, of course, curiosity got the better of my friend and she opened the envelope.

Inside it told the story of the true father of my friend. The man who raised her, whom she had known as her father, was in fact not her biological father. So she had just lost her mother and now her mother's lies were threatening to destroy her. This meant also that her 'father' had lied to her as well. He had passed on years before so she couldn't even address the situation with him.

Once the grief of death settled and the business of her mother's estate was finalized, she began the search for her biological father. She found him, just months after he died. The lie of her mother was years in the making an involved other family members.

If you have a problem with making lies, I have a question for you to ask yourself. "Why do I lie?"

Ask yourself, or better yet, ask God to reveal to you, the root cause of your telling of lies. When and why did the lying spirit come into your life? Was it generational? Did your parent(s) lie? Is it situational? Did you suffer some trauma and you thought you had to start lying in order to survive?

Do you have lies you have made that are waiting to destroy someone? With Jesus, you can take care of them now. Repent before the Lord. Ask for strategy to tear down the lies and make things right with the least damage to others. Meet Jesus.

12 WHEN I WAS DRUNK

I have to laugh at this chapter. You see, my husband was never addicted to anything in his life. He only tried drugs once or twice and his drinking was social drinking, not alcoholism. But as a Christian, when he thought about the times he did drink too much, he was mortified.

You see, when we give our minds over to drugs and alcohol to the point of intoxication, we cannot serve God properly. We become foolish an ineffectual.

There is a term 'drunk in the Holy Spirit', which I don't like. We say it because we don't know how else to describe the feeling we have when Holy Spirit overwhelms us.

There is another reason not to lose control of our senses. God says, "Be sober, be vigilant; because your adversary the devil, as a roaring lion, walks about, seeking whom he may devour:" (1 Peter 5:8)

Yes, I realize 'sober' means to get serious minded, but it's hard to be serious minded when you are drunk or high.

Now, I am not legalistic concerning the Word of God. I know from my study of scripture, we are permitted some wine, but not to the point of inebriation.

There are many stories of conversion during intoxication. One famous singer told of meeting Jesus while crawling on the bathroom floor licking up spilled cocaine.

If Jesus can deliver the demoniac full of devils as we read in the gospels, I suppose Jesus can certainly deliver someone who is high or drunk. Hurting people are hurting people. They need the love of their Savior.

Some people report that, after salvation, they lost all desire for alcohol or drugs. Others simply give up what is illegal anyway and tone down the drinking. The point is more Jesus and less substitutes.

Being drunk or high are usually something to mask pain. They mask past and potential pain. We can see a young girl who doesn't feel loved, desired, or pretty. This hurts and she drinks too much to cover the hurt. She also drinks too much because she is about to give herself to a stranger thinking the sex shows she is pretty and someone somebody wants to be with.

Of course, this activity hurts her because somewhere inside she knows this is false love and that she is debasing herself. So she drinks more to numb the feeling of self-loathing. The man she is with may be drunk and high for the same reason.

What these two need is to meet Jesus, the one who *does* truly love them. Jesus desires them. Jesus sees them as beautiful in their potential as children of God.

I also want to take an opportunity here to address the industries of psychology and medicine. Sometimes we can be so smart we are stupid. We make simple things complicated. Instead of fixing the root of addiction and setting the person free, we label them for life.

It breaks my heart when I see a Christian who is delivered from the past, functioning very well in Christ Jesus, but still considers themselves a 'recovering alcoholic'. What a horrible label. Whom the Son sets free is free indeed! You are healed by the stripes of Christ. You are not recovering, you are recovered! Throw off man's labels. Take on God's decrees over you.

Only Jesus can take away the past events that have scarred us and caused us to over indulge, to become drunk and high way too many times.

In the brain fog of intoxication, it is Jesus who comes walking toward us with love in His eyes and outstretched arms, not condemning, not condoning, but with the desire to take away our pain.

Meet Jesus.

13 WHEN I WAS POOR

Jesus said, "I came that they might have life and that more than abundant." (John 10:10)

He also spoke of those who were poor in spirit and said that the poor are always among us. Of course, when we say we are poor, we mean we don't have enough money. However, being poor is an attitude, not a tangible condition.

John the Baptist roamed around eating bugs and wearing uncomfortable clothing, but he wasn't poor. He was rich in purpose. There were rich people in the Bible who did not live in fancy houses, but wandered the desert. Adam and Eve did not possess money, but certainly were rich before their sin tripped them up.

Yes, poor is state of mind. Not being able the rent or buy food is a need. God said God would supply all our need according to riches in glory by Christ Jesus. (Philippians 4:19)

I will admit that sometimes God is just barely on time with the supply and the supply is sometimes just barely enough in my earthly estimation, but God never fails in supplying. It does seem God takes delight in supplying some way other than the way we want. As long as God supplies, it's ok.

God is faithful.

When we feel destitute, we are in perfect position for God to show up and show off. An example is found in a time my husband and I were headed toward poverty.

Due to some political maneuvering by a company we both worked for, we found ourselves without jobs. It happened without warning. We were working and the next hour, we were unemployed. At the time, we had the bad habit of living paycheck to paycheck. We didn't save money. We played with money.

We weren't sure what to do, but we had just begun to live Christian lives so something told us to go talk to our Pastor. Our Pastor got a revelation from the Lord that we should start our own business. We would not have thought of that one. However, that meant an extended period of time with no income.

By faith, we did start our own business. Sure enough, we were what we considered poor. During this time, God began to teach us about His supply.

We had a freezer with some leftovers from a butchered cow in the very bottom, but it was the parts we really didn't want to eat. We ate them anyway. And we were thankful.

I was out of laundry detergent, but hadn't thrown the container away. I thought I would just put some water in the bottle, swish it around and use it. However clean the laundry came out, that would be it until we could afford more.

When I picked up what I knew was an empty bottle, IT WAS FULL! God had made a miracle. I washed clothes with that detergent for a long time until we could afford more. It was like the cruse of oil in the Bible.

We went to church one Sunday and when the offering plate was passed all we had was seven dollars and no other money coming in. We faithfully put the seven dollars in the plate, trusting the Lord. Seven dollars wasn't going to solve the problem by itself. It must be seed for a harvest. The next day there was an unexpected check in the mail for seven hundred dollars.

God is faithful.

Usually when we think we don't have enough, we actually have a lot. In working with ministers from third world countries, I have learned what true poverty looks like. They may not eat for days. They may not have a place to live. They have no way to get medical help. They can't afford to send children to school. They are truly poor in finances and things, but rich in the Lord.

We need to meet Jesus and understand how much we have in Him. He became poor so that we might become rich. The richness may not be in financial wealth or it may be that. We just need to be thankful and see things through His eyes.

Meet Jesus in your poverty. God is faithful.

One writer in scripture said he had never seen the righteous forsaken nor his seed begging for bread. (Ps 37:25)

When we belong to God, we are joint heirs of the kingdom. He will take care of us. God is faithful.

DR. LINDA KAY SMITH

EPILOGUE

This book is closure for me. My husband left me this outline and I trust I have done it justice. Only time will tell.

Each chapter is personal and individual to the reader. What it meant to you, I cannot say. I hope the few words on each subject brought clarity and comfort.

What I do know is that you and I need Jesus. To that end, I offer this prayer. I hope, if you've never accepted the Lord Jesus Christ as *your* personal Lord and Savior, you will do so now. Meet Jesus.

"Father God, I want your Son, Jesus, to be my Lord. I believe that You raised Him from the dead. Jesus, come into my heart and live in and through me. I thank you for forgiving me of all my sin, cleansing me from unrighteousness. Thank you for saving me. I pray in the name of Jesus. Amen"

DR. LINDA KAY SMITH

ABOUT THE AUTHOR

Dr. Linda Smith – Christian, pastor, teacher, author, minister and wife. In partnership with her husband, Robert, she co-founded Free Them Ministries, Inc., an international Christian outreach. Together they also pastor PowerHouse Christian Center in San Marcos, Texas. Dr. Smith was ordained into the ministry of Jesus Christ in 1981 with a directive from God to set the captives free from their pasts, their false assumptions concerning God and His word, and the emotional barriers that have been placed between people and God.

With an earned Ph.D. in Theology, and a gift for teaching, Linda presents the dynamic word of God in a way that personalizes the message for the hearer. Students come away from Dr. Smith's classes with an excitement for the word of God and an ability to find out for themselves the meaning of the scriptures. Dr. Smith has served the church for over thirty years educating people of all ages with the Word of God. She has also served on the faculty board of Christian universities and was the Christian Education Director in several churches across America.

Linda uses the Bible, humor and her testimony to exhort the people of God seek a more intimate walk with the Lord Jesus Christ. Her ministry is a mandate to create spiritual maturity and integrity in churches, businesses and homes with anointed messages that glorify God Almighty. This minister of God is Holy Spirit filled and has a sincere desire in her heart for the Bride of Christ to be fully prepared for marriage to the Bridegroom.

As an author, Dr. Smith's books and other literature have appeared in a variety of magazines including *Charisma*, *Spirit Led Woman*, and *Christian Women Today*. Her first book, *God's Wife, the Bride of Christ*, has been distributed world-wide.

To schedule this dynamic speaker, contact Free Them Ministries, Inc. Please visit the ministry website at www.freethem.org.

www.ingramcontent.com/pod-product-compliance
Lightning Source LLC
Chambersburg PA
CBHW061345040426
42444CB00011B/3087